Michelle Moloney King

ANOTHER WORD FOR MOTHER

SV

SurVision Books

First published in 2022 by
SurVision Books
Dublin, Ireland
Reggio di Calabria, Italy
www.survisionmagazine.com

Copyright © Michelle Moloney King, 2022
Cover image © Michelle Moloney King, 2022
Design © SurVision Books, 2022

ISBN: 978-1-912963-31-7

This book is in copyright. No part of this publication may be reproduced, stored in a retrieval system, or transmitted in any form or by any means without the prior permission in writing from the publisher.

Acknowledgments

Grateful acknowledgment is made to the editors of the following, in which some of these poems, or versions of them, originally appeared:

Penteract Press, 3:AM, M58, Streetcake Magazine, Babel Journal, Mercurious Press, Full House Lit, Strukturriss Journal

I would like to acknowledge the support from the poets and readers of Beir Bua Press and a special thanks to my husband for the time to write and the work. Thanks to Féileacáin Ireland for the memory box; I am eternally grateful.

For Regan and Dylan King
Born Friday 13th, 2018. A lucky day for us all.

Contents

Part I. Almost Narrative

Image of Reality TV in Neon	5
"Hello!"	6
Bad Dreams Accidently Becoming	8
Painted-Up Front Door	9
Truck – Here, There but Not Everywhere!	10
The Flying Face of Melted Clocks	12
Piano and T	14
Toddlers Can Have Big Mushrooms Too	16
And If Time Can Travel with Us Then Why Couldn't He	18
On the Quantum Poetics of Loss	20

Part II. Play

High Art and a Closed Gallery with Security Guarded Entrances	22
As Munich as Possible	23
Modifiable Stories	24
On Having My Back	25
Sweet Sunday Child	26
Green Tomato-less Sofas	28
Yummy Mummy	29
A Study on Maps	30
Don't Start Sentences with a Verb	31
America Championed the Impressionists, Huzzah!	32
Paris Cafe Culture Is Lost in Rural Ireland Due to Broken GPS	33
Self-Portrait of News and Fresh Wine	34
A Homestead Fire	35
×+×÷111223211	36
City Yoga Code	37
Transfer Deadline Day Goes Swish Swish Swish	38
No, Go Away Bucket	39
Everyone Is a Holiday Cottage	40

Part I. Almost Narrative

Image of Reality TV in Neon

Having taken the isotopic raster printed image and you
dipping from pigment, pressing one by one;
an alpha ray running after a beta ray.
You,
as if incomplete and fragmented
the disturbance of an observed system
by the act of observation – dot by dot.

    The assumption endures
as if the nuclei of radioactivity and Picasso's personal therapist are
dancing once again.
Never corrected or extracted y
our photographic image of the modern world
after lockdown but before being filtered – new wine into old bottles

Yesterday, a cartoon hero with shopping hauls explored the printed
image
      As it contorts the astral rays of the decay chain,
      As it morphs slowly into a gold-leaf electroscope,
      As it accelerators into a particle bubble chamber

– Please connect the dots up close and personal in time for last year's
brunch meeting.

"Hello!"

Pre-Surgery / Operating Table – Early Morning

She makes shhh gestures at two swans flying past and
prays to start. Around the bed, they refer vaguely to
'extra measures.'
Seven dials and debating already.

    Debating people who hum to cover smoke alarms.
    Debating imaginary solutions where exceptions are the rule
    Debating our shared fourth dimension and how to translate it
to prose.

Or metaphor.
Or baby food.
      Or a miracle because that what's it's become about now.
           Debating the power of language – prelanguage.

But no one sees the vision just what is there in front of them.

If it's on paper then it must be true,
If the computers shots out results
then we do X
until Y is meat or met.

But what of spontaneous,
microscopic swerving of atoms in

  space as they fall in a vertical path?
       "See a different path!"

Pre-Surgery / Operating Table – Late Morning

With my 2 hours left, they decide on the word of the day:
"Umbrage": meaning unrequited hunger.
                              ANAESTHETISED
There never is any warning.
light fades.
to grow, sprout, spread. Stirs it in.
Are we sure it's malfunctioning, and not just becoming self-aware?
Financial freedom is a lie.
So glad you're here, a battalion of friends have arrived
to taste?
lend hands in twos – welding copper crowns.
While I'm outside, children, get baking! You've met! 'Course you have.
We say, "trick-acting!"
They think of how religions can take new and surprising forms with large amounts of irrigation and pesticide to maintain yields. It's all going plant-based.
Big paper smiles. Don't tell anyone about the Your hidden history –
underlined.
secret ingredient.
And another thing…
gold can grow on Eucalyptus trees.

Bad Dreams Accidently Becoming

vegetables, such as carrots or spuds, can become monumental
so-in-sos, as if knowing the primordial mass of baby
is in a state of needing or comprehending.
Waiting,
by incandescent writings
by pataphysic imaginary solutions,
by inaugural performances of unfurling potential.

Moving onwards through falling houses,
climbing sideways on ice cream mountains,
and crawling on sunshine floors.

Our first job, is to create a garland
to decorate the jumping salmon fireplace
    with gargoyles of biblical purple,
    with old dreams
        posthumously laid bare and needing to be expunged,
    with the knowledge of how unspoken and unlearnt
        can harm,
    with dreams of lazy days made new with only
        positive outcomes,
    with incendiary hopes and nothing left to chance.

Adoring the short and holding space as witness
to the hazards of hospitals
masquerading as hotels for exiguous diagnostics
and can you blame the dreamer not knowing to fake it and then it is made?
Notice this. Notice
this in a particular way. And pay no heed to the internal. – *I wonder...*

Painted-Up Front Doors

You can't truck around with mushrooms – chopping onions;

leading to crying
leading to irresponsible trajectories
of uncritical thinking,
leading to the predecessors' darkened waters
with no shade,
leading to our eyes
responsible for the creation of matter – of life.

No more.

    No more hiding from Heisenberg's uncertainty principle.
    No more hiding from sincere hydrodynamics
        of hungry turbulent flows.
    No more hiding from the waltzing
      atomic nucleus and cosmic rays
          only the powerful creator's vessel can hold.

    No more hiding from The Eyes seeing into you and finding you lacking
or worse

No matter –
They lead into a quick waltz around the room and talk of definitions: To take umbrage," to feel slighted in barely one generation.

She thinks the answer will come from the forests themselves.
   – To take offence for "shade" and the scene goes on.

Blue canto muck, spellbound with mudrooms – stirring reunions.

Truck – Here, There but Not Everywhere!

Every morning I wake up I win the lotto and collect my classic
utilitarian identity before dumping my personal preferences,
    as if waiting on a microwave bing to
        cultivate the right character traits
    as if Kings keeping the dutiful behaviours
        stored in a kitchen cupboard.
    as if falling down bunny holes
        of proper normative ethos
        of baby groups and talks of men's interests – always sport
disguised as the meal of the day.

There, by the buggy tree,
we step over playdough, woolly hats, and ignore the nodding of
Moral Agents.

Near the waving curtains,
the closed winking windows focus on morality.

Here birds nest.
Across from empty nighttimes of flying
   and gathering,
    turning and snapping
        with hedonic calculus – we kneel in the nearby lake of new
breathing,
     and know,
we can no longer use an adjective
to modify a noun now that it refers
to a distance no mother can transverse.

We are not really up for much anymore and no one takes the time to ask why.

>READER: "Is she available for motivational speaking?"

The Flying Face of Melted Clocks

Is this your Dada too? If so, do you know where he is buried?
Where his optical cubist dreams have washed to?
Where his iridescent longing
for an unknown guide interrupting the path has Shaman-ed to?

Such hyperbolic zeal for an
invisible universe to
       see us.

Him,
       with his black sheep hair,
       cyanotype and prismatic eyes,
Him,
       with his chrysalis children,
Him,
       with a singular secular possession for
       the malintended multiverse and the waiting
        butterflies mistranslated as an artificial idiom.
Him,
       as a branched organisation willing to create understanding
       and a shared vision with no lexicon to verb it.

Always monologuing with your network of peers
bending the knee to an unknown 4th person narrative as if knowing
more than the rest of us
    and yet
    nothing happening.

A stuckness / A sickness.
A desert ecosystem forming where once was a kitchen table.

The Old Guard is ebbing out.

Our reality and self, constructed through a language of the chicory heart.

We come in the name of the Lord to elicit our likeness in His name.

Exit. Yard. Nighttime.

Piano and T

If you haven't been acclimatising then do not go in – WAIT

    for the bacterial mats and mosses to quantum leap
    for the lichens and fungi to form a new heart layer
    for the stars to refuel and the vanished reappear
    for the flash flooding of an agricultural collapse.

Our loved one.
    One time seal,
        our ocean panther; It's a mask – not a face.

We weep at the flood's edge
only in darkness,
only in the uniform of the
    criminally positive, the damned, the doomed and the soon to be
forgotten into tricking we go on forever.

We've got a cocktail party to throw: Against a wall.

So let's construct soufflés
made of microclimate
    epiphytes and
        lithophytes,
made of filmy ferns,
made of a colonised slab of rock
    eeked from our memories of the evaporated.

The machines we build cannot deal with an apprehend!
Just the worship of plastic aided by a celebration of desertification

as it watches fish jumping out of the sea to perceive the waves,
   as it savagely swims beneath a fountain of emeralds
   as it is known and then unknown,

   gone – an aunt's wrinkly tanned smile rubbed out and we are left with
   a glossary of atoms.
     She was a force that opens suns, what hope have I?

Toddlers Can Have Big Mushrooms Too

But first, we paint the scene and noun it until we are cement:
After everything that's happened the flagellated sixty
non-funeral guests eat wild mushrooms.
Frozen obituary rain is blending well with eukaryotic botany while
a slight inconvenience of spatially,
    monophyletic temporally,
    and taxonomical modally is a
        wave function collapsing.

My imagination and the semantic values of constituents and the
ceremony begin – join us in slow motion of high rates. But can it
cleave us free?
All that I am, ever was, in the beginning
or acknowledging what
can't actually be taken... as if a slow acceptance of suffering.

I think we're not supposed to talk about meta-language right now
nor
tracing it out over mountain spectres
of thawed plastic
quenching a volcano of digital bytes to photons.
    Digital prayers.
    And no one seeing the light show.
    Nor, outlining it before the feet
        of Pagan urns
        of natal despondency.

    Loss.

Ashes to ashes – myxomycetes
While a heart is jumping ship from the principal decomposers.
Nor, sketching it against a modal auxiliary with Banksy as a
backdrop, oh, if we could only photosynthesize.
Those of us assigning interpretations of semantic values or
extensions relative to a point in time
        may need to drop the subject of this fame.
Those tumultuous fungi eventually eat the funeral non-guests and
you who lived as dressed kinesiology warned others of empty
vessels, you who stopped suns, we now watch your wake on a
Youtube live while we meditate at a juncture of internal war played
out at the dialectic of a poo-can.

And If Time Can Travel with Us Then Why Couldn't He

Come home A backward looking dog Those skys No
acknowledgement in life and how alike you are to the late great
artists My picture perfect, landscape of your eyes Canvas shroud Off
all this earthy beauty In death
celebrated and curated Quintessential loss passed off as normal Can
you paint that for him, do what Constable did for all the sleeping
babas Shhh
 "In your own time, god's work, hey, there are others" Taken on a
journey into shamans and saints roundabouts Too short, lungs and
tree of life failed There is you and then there is You. Single-handedly,
before the doors open, authentic enough for instance on
breaking rules Painter of light, premie mortality Even Kings
evaporate into logos or light
2 days
Lifecycle with no experiential plight. Floating feet. Please touch the ground.
- Yellow!
- The Beatles
- The number 3
- Bob Dylan
- Little King
- UL
- On the steps near the library
- NYC
- Vegas
- The Palace
- You and your brother

Training will ruin us all on the meditation of death Ignorance on fire, gone home little rule breaker

No training, enthusiasm Head South A variety of subtle tsunami subjects will come to you via travel Here is a place where the moon dances tangos with ploughs and stars are still Paper barriers are to be burned One is never ready to cross Is it ever enough? My great heroes as big as sugar bags How thin the vale using art stepping stones to tuck you in
We wait for you by the pumpkin patch, purple unicorn shovels and a warm sandpit ready

On the Quantum Poetics of Loss

I'm interested to know if people become
mangled in tabloid poetics of
biographical nuclear narrative with chapters that connect
      themes, obsessions, and
        undercurrents

before realising roles in The Carnival of Being.
      Is the anecdote "Ubu roi"
      and can it be augmented?

We
have choices –
      Beyond the human-centric and design thinking
      through the acrylic paintings of
         spectroscopy
      beneath the states of bound or vapour – our wet lives are slowly
drying.

Where were her choices?

Or are we destined to hide our faining errors to
the clash of the classes with borders of fake togetherness.

I am revelled in seeing who we always were, each choice defining a life,
Do we continue reading back in privileged horror at what
the suited rules
whisper?

Brought to the edge of performance –
ontology over epistemology
being over knowing
or hydrogenicly bound to the life's fabric before circulating as
vapour in the void.
A life's work 1940 – 2022
diffused and the dynamics between the two states
a matter of air-flow   e v a p o r a t i n g –

Part II. Play

High Art and a Closed Gallery with Security Guarded Entrances

Below us, the blue city,
it's almost like creating life
moulding gummy bears in fibreglass.
In the desert kingdom, critics and artists are hemmed together
and all the while longing to dethrone the empire before belonging
to it.

Hollow cavities of the desired shape
Never incognito argumentations
stifle his hyphenated-identities of sweltering phylogenetic analysis
looping in our minds
as if assuming the happy reaper.

Ensconce the sculptors behind their desks.
Work on them in transit, if needed
  As if your life depended on it
  As if a bioactive, late Dadaist clock
  As if a plural noun with no singular.

Piece by piece, oh the finery of square heads and electronic
pointers.
A warm glow/ A warmer globe.

And you who inherit the garret mind, the underground quakes of
angel bridges and the ghosts cast in cement, please
go ask them why, living artist.

As Munich as Possible

A greyhound is held hostage at the top of a page by a crooked washing powder pyramid. They demand archival data for its safe return. The title has to do with being blackmailed / Blackbeard.

"There's comfort forming in the ashes of stars," said the dog.
Despite the shock of initial grief, to moderate
heat and influence. Who is "we" again?

The day before next Christmas, I'd written the story behind
quests, and yet I laughed, or will do so, at her, while a stray hind leg scratches a nose.
The power you need is in the rings of dust six months after the title "galaxies begotten from a matter cavity" is released.

Come clean on a bus once again a million years ago. It's way too soon
for a bemused stranger's morphology. My latest request is
that ye listen to the richer mutt in practice mode.

The facilities realised I was lightly summoning and slipping into school and
I can still remember the shock. And so I left,
aghast at evolved cavemen and the celestial building materials on parade, can we not chase wigs in peace!
Feel its velvet tongue on the back of your neck and
pet it anyway while my owners walk their child until "As Munich as Possible" prevails again.

Modifiable Stories

Chuckle at my left hand, maybe,
no luck with rose buds blooming and a
hover in my right hand sucking up the clay.
"I can't judge anyone anymore," Doctor!
They're some metamorphosis/ back at work, thanks anyway.
And I moved right into casual planes
feeling that it might be
a phoney Mom, as I knew her.

"Can I ask you a question, Yellow Digger?"
As we linger nearby in trust, please
give me a chance. While sitting against
imaginary walls sound good so do
cafeteria coffee plants.
Leave it to me to tell her a few weeks before, celebrate now.
Sitting outside kitchens the chickens can be cooked
your way, in the outback. Which changes things
considering the sprinkles / will someone think
of the sprinkles?

On Having My Back

Put him away to the side of the can.
Talk about luck,
it changes your name. Wearing two sun
hats to turn the storeroom
into a friend's library. Next thing
to do for this bust parent
arrested and tested is...

Did you turn the stables into a
boating mouse at home, my darling?
I could not / will not look,
Wednesday, you're welcome.

I'm back, you spell falafel
with a sour strawberry pop tart.
We're all here together
in spam
and that's really special;
no longer sitting on that cake.
Sure!
The work was close to his heart.

It just gets better and better to find the
Haute exhibition. Survival mood and
more tests, I dunno.
To being booked out all summer and
not getting
ahead in horse-slips – the link is alive?

Sweet Sunday Child

Capture the ever-changing nature of society layers
thinking they are street fashion. Telling comments of real sensations
the birth of double taps and washing hands. Both changing and
following safe cryogenic rules contribute to diffusers of lemon. It's
about class.

Go teach one. No thanks, I'm immensely inspired not to be
commonplace. At this exact spot so many awed by the spending views
of ruffled
lace. It might look very peaceful taking place on a Monday.
See, the less fortunate travel for ice-cream
trucks. I play about seven
characters celebrating the nominated losses. No small undertaking.
Look for the ugly, not interesting, by empty glasses. Our free
consultation is easy to do something by work montage. Cure to-do lists
with lotto tickets. It has
already been won.
Explore
for thousands of miles, go online, move each kernel –
pebble by pebble in a fish mouth, one click after another.

Are you going to disappoint them or not.
Immerse yourself in new archives. You have got to believe.
An equine artist serves us all well.

That Belfast
lady urges you to end belief in the circus.
Walk in the step of elephant circles.

Position remaining the same, assemble faux coup. The hum of the
        diffuser lulling you
to wake up in dreams.
Inherit your mama's yawn.

Green Tomato-less Sofas

Battery life can be extended – reads the sign at the kindred
Chemists' open-air market.
It always helps to be a little bit broken.
They sell gold in his local bookies, above liquid hope.

I don't belong here, said the American, mad at being
shushed by the local sleeping babes in Irish cows' arms.
"Who does he be always long in the face?"
 Let's blame graffiti giraffes and Jackeens.

Say 'Nathin!

Yummy Mummy

The milk has churned and left on its heels, pivoting
at the last sonic wave goodbye, the baby refused to share a
high five and is reported to have cried,
"You Sir, are a quitter."
The role, played by *the mummy*, was replaced
and a more flatter version installed, alluringly said,
"Ta ta to the milk."
Dada, sources close to the family stage have
whispered, gave the baby an employability bowl of
dry cereal with salty water.
The lullaby owl laughed at their breakfast
offerings to *The Baby*
while the cupboard mice have left the building citing
irreconcilable differences to a local squinting window.
The pictures for Instagram however look of
familial bliss.

A Study on Maps

I'm going to take you on a
journey, rolling
into history completely
transformed,
follow in the footsteps of
dandelions. Utterly
hooked, the can grow
anywhere. Cracks in your
mind,
simplistic and childlike. You are just as significant
closeted away, this is St. Anthony.
Considered motifs craft your
life story as a sailing boat.
Have you found a harbour
yet? Just smile, old boy,
never knowing, you were a fisherman, not the captain.

Don't Start Sentences with a Verb

Recall the things you took. This is someone who is making sense of it. Quintessential adventures of seagulls, crying your bare name. Remember when the railways arrived, our elders had freedom. Holding your train now, smartphone traveller. Walk through our most important works, oh, the cobbled back streets of life's journey. "Man's mercifulness to man."

Become significant to wolves. Clever is considered simple. Every nice village I travel to I buy a home. Weary traveller, home is where the heart is longing.
Are you copying then not seeing? Take to the high seas, maybe the walrus can point you onwards. Because it does leave a scarf, at the mercy of your uncharted heart.

Storm against those rocks, a modest scale of life's library room. Up close, the jolly and holys. I love it. Because it's personal, a life's story sorry told in inks, chalks, and pigments. That's the highest work we leave behind. Transport and transmit your loquacious magic. On the edge of cliff train journeys, hanging on, pupils wide. The architecture of views and yous. Are we iconic yet/ Mundane celebrated as significance? Wow!

America Championed the Impressionists, Huzzah!

The Chapel on the hill, his blue eyes fishing,
   eternity marking down points of inspiration.
To paint or write down is to capture. The wild street galleries of chairs
   and kitchen tables. Anchor me in tea time. And toast.
to the bird's-eye view of 2020. Hindsight of the fantastic
   seal clap. Essentially, we retrace footsteps of the good
and great, overlooking the light of nowness.
   Burritos transporting us to the terrors of the sea.

Painting a cathartic leaking onto canvas informs
   me of your story. Dealing out traumas dressed up
in pigments. Life ahoy! Come home. Was your
   life safer on stage?
You can be a disentangled age.
   The coves are reaching for you now.
Amphitheatres embrace in a time of pirates, smugglers and wreckers.

I manage the lookout station, on the wildling coast of your
   toddler group. Return to me in your art even
handprint, finger print works will evoke you.

Time is not money. Time is art.
   The god is in all of us. A holy view. It was always the
      uneducated that changed history, sweetly plotting new maps.
      Bullseye of a mind gone   **a w r y.**

Paris Cafe Culture Is Lost in Rural Ireland Due to Broken GPS

One sees those skys all the time, 200 years later
and still stepping into landscapes,
do they want to share the same connections with us? Setting up the specious microcosm of our work,
a different side to usual views. Farmlands of canvas
with no painters to be found honest and we all know that
if you wish to post outside of these guidelines then
you need a purpose.

The student's thing is to retreat from the margin.
Celebrating the ordinary, an art history museum broke open.
Bye-bye stale Kings. Farmers wondering when I am here.

Beyond analysis now saving the villages from living life in aspic,
the trees are my family. Normal people cooking, eating and cleaning celebrated.

The acceptance of an end to torment becomes a gothic loss and always the perfect backdrop for art and always the promise of each coming season delight and the founder will also have a friendly, comfortable atmosphere to help with a nudge, available at all times.

What do you see in the cloud?. Sky god in gliders. Touch. Fly through. Old testament rainbows, You are my tallest spire.

Self-Portrait of News and Fresh Wine

Today, I want to take you into a
painting of walls, dulling minds too full to practice mindfulness, is it less we need.
With great detail.
An extraordinary artist. All the complexity of Ginsberg pink clouds. A rambunctious character on stage, ops should that be page or canvas.
Nice placement you have here.
Over here an artist those in the nos and yes adored.
It wasn't the usual philosophical visitors

Look closer, the painting is frozen and resonating off the surface of the things.
Someone coming in the 1850s pressed forward into Google.
An informative canvas.
Christ? Did they just say you want to be stored in your subconscious?

Round two of our first walk
An urban farm selling fish and chips.
And finally, we will venture the dark alleys on Instagram.
Sometimes going to 2 or 3 plays a day.
The market opening up, give mama a kiss.

A Homestead Fire

                      As it burnt down he sat in the pub opposite
    A man drinking waaain in front of his own fire
 The place to come home to
                one of your favourite buildings of cave paintings.
Sat. Transfixed by it. Transfixed by it. Transfixed by it. Transfixed by it. Transfixed by it.
      There is a narrative falling out and falling up
        into cosmetic clouds.
            The loss of virtue, decoupled from rude society.
              A whole day eatin' & plenty of sandwiches left
            and right of street corners.

    You and I have the same taste.
   'Cause not to paint beautiful scenes is
  well, don't know if there's integrity in smoky house hugs.

×+×÷111223211

A chief meeting has gathered in Brussels
by my aubergines.
A methodology of working out this account
taken by a snapshot,
"There ya go mister!"

Worried about the delay of offers, you complain.
Victim hoodies swapped out for hero capes
while a special committee hearing was excavated by capacity.

Did you take action lately?

We have everything
you need. Patchy rain now, the best way to take a
shower of flowers frowning to an empty clothesline.
Get a taste for the abnormal life.

City Yoga Code

Dolls were used to represent spirits in my past. Measuring heartbeats, I asked us to spy on a menagerie of dolls on a fireplace mantel, with binoculars, while taking the pulse of the person next to you. Someone doing this said, "This is sensory overload." And it is. Taking the living, thumping pulse of someone while carefully studying a community of dolls animates the moment.

Distraction leads to going to your inner self. This is a blueprint of who we are at the time of writing it. Oh, the many seaweedy mysteries of the sea. The canvas and her colours are dipping toes in elegance and my hair, I recognise as antennas. And the noise...blackboard scratching, Halloween hugging. Your words – as sharp as HB pencil on recycled yellow legal pages. Now, all we need is someone to write it down. Hi, will you take notes below, thanks:

_____
_____
_____
_____
_____
_____
_____
_____
_____
_____
_____
_____
_____
_____
_____

Transfer Deadline Day Goes Swish Swish Swish

There are v.v.v.v. many people who fear this is the end of their leeks, which are always handy for the ploughman salad. Jobbers and businesses are in tears tonight for the want of a believer. My people on the other advisory body only did that to surprise the wheels on the red truck tractor which the smoking lady economically ate, if you will, and that ain't love, mate. Eh?

Chairs would be fired in normal times, all for the need of unwanted carrots by the ringing doorbell. It's really important the event goes well for us, without a witch, because it's all about retaliation and Swiss watches. It's a double edged sword for a breadman deemed not worthy of shelves. It's been a hard year, sister and if something dramatic happens to the mice in my kitchen then it justifies a nuclear option and then (and only then) do you talk to the priest, not the press! You got a guarantee for this life?

No, Go Away Bucket

Put the baby in the duck water,
it's a good place for hyper'alarms. I read
the newspaper on a cold chocolate day-fall
and it was far from peri-peri.

"You were raised to just eat its food,
and its labourers," said the waitress.
There's probably not only one way to
 find out but I'll turn the water on anyway.

Mummy is a way for stars. Umm, that time
machine? Yummy.
The yard is too full of trucks today,
rake your tractor out to help the
crow doctor more.

There's always too many
blackbirds in town, today of all
days, come on in and I'll fall before
the working doors of my poems for
her. Under our sun hats, you can
find an honest night watchwoman
and a short-sleeved smile.

Everyone Is a Holiday Cottage

A new way of seeing, the lack in you
is the way. Unlearn. Shake the school
out of your hair, the memory of imagination.
His yellow plastic coat shines from where brass lions once sat,
the multifarious fire humming cerulean smoke screens.
I see you see through cyan-coloured printed eyes, the best blueprint.

Can I place my hands nearer to scoop your
face from the compendious catalogue?
Mothers will always be
there in your heart, ubiquitous love
while you run both routes
simultaneously as if polyphonic with crisscrossing couplets,
as if forgetting the quasiparticles of the adjacent anyones,
as if letting the paths run wild.

It's just that we ought not to paint – beautiful summer
evenings but the longest weekend of our winter.
The sun will look out and fall down a little screwy in
a convex mirror with the rest of the poem in unmusical
terms when we were lost and all the better for it.

Selected Poetry Titles Published by SurVision Books

Seeds of Gravity: An Anthology of Contemporary Surrealist Poetry from Ireland
Edited by Anatoly Kudryavitsky
ISBN 978-1-912963-18-8

Noelle Kocot. *Humanity*
(New Poetics: USA)
ISBN 978-1-9995903-0-7

Ciaran O'Driscoll. *The Speaking Trees*
(New Poetics: Ireland)
ISBN 978-1-9995903-1-4

Ciaran O'Driscoll. *Angel Hour*
ISBN 978-1-912963-27-0

Helen Ivory. *Maps of the Abandoned City*
(New Poetics: England)
ISBN 978-1-912963-04-1

John W. Sexton. *Inverted Night*
(New Poetics: Ireland)
ISBN 978-1-912963-05-8

Afric McGlinchey. *Invisible Insane*
(New Poetics: Ireland)
ISBN 978-1-9995903-3-8

Anatoly Kudryavitsky. *Stowaway*
(New Poetics: Ireland)
ISBN 978-1-9995903-2-1

Tim Murphy. *The Cacti Do Not Move*
(New Poetics: Ireland)
ISBN 978-1-912963-07-2

Tony Kitt. *The Magic Phlute*
(New Poetics: Ireland)
ISBN 978-1-912963-08-9

Matthew Geden. *Fruit*
(New Poetics: Ireland)
ISBN 978-1-912963-16-4

Marc Vincenz. *Einstein Fledermaus*
(New Poetics: USA)
ISBN 978-1-912963-20-1

Tony Bailie. *Mountain Under Heaven*
(Winner of James Tate Poetry Prize 2019)
ISBN 978-1-912963-09-6

Alison Dunhill. *As Pure as Coal Dust*
(Winner of James Tate Poetry Prize 2020)
ISBN 978-1-912963-23-2

Aoife Mannix. *Alice under the Knife*
(Winner of James Tate Poetry Prize 2020)
ISBN 978-1-912963-26-3

Charles Borkhuis. *Spontaneous Combustion*
(Winner of James Tate Poetry Prize 2021)
ISBN 978-1-912963-30-0

George Kalamaras. *Through the Silk-Heavy Rains*
ISBN 978-1-912963-28-7

Order our books from https://survisionmagazine.com/bookshop.htm

www.ingramcontent.com/pod-product-compliance
Lightning Source LLC
Chambersburg PA
CBHW061307040426
42444CB00010B/2553